Lessons of Water & Thirst

Richard Fammerée

COLLAGE PRESS

CHICAGO
2000

Some of these poems have appeared in
The Spoon River Poetry Review, Opus Literary Review, Pegasus, Knowing Stones: Poems of Exotic Places, The Oyez Review and
The Avon Literary Intelligencer (Bath, England).

Special thanks to Linnaeus and Jeff Helgeson for their careful reading of this text in manuscript.

R.F.

Printed in the United States of America.

Art Direction: Christopher Waldemar Kowal
& Kate Hoddinott

Cover Design:
Christopher Waldemar Kowal,
Kate Hoddinott & Richard Fammerée

Photographs:
Linnaeus by Paul Natkin
Fammerée by G. Reid Skjervold

Collage Press
P.O. Box 1904
Chicago, IL 60690-1904

ISBN 0-9615879-5-4

for my family in every incarnation

for Robert & Miranda

with warmest regards
to fellow pilgrims of light,

Richard

9/02

Each of us awakes from the truth of dreams
to the lives of our own making.

Ephemerae

I could not sleep while you slept.
Any little animal might have sheltered
in your body; and I kept
leaves from your eyes and things from your hair until
your lips revived, bending
back my fingers to the lessons
of water and thirst. Fires that night
digested the wet, and when their long viridian became
your arms and a delirium
became our legs, threads
relinquished us, and we were not puppeted
by earth, and we were not puppeted
by heaven. We became
larger than form and texture and scent—
something like clouds—and fear was driven
from the manger of our bellies, and anger's thin lips
could not diminish us. We ate everything
that was red,
and everything that was red
was delicious. My sap was greening
your milky body, then your legs slapped. They slapped
into fins and you arced
and my chin and
ear separated, and silver and more silver and silver
again, I quivered behind you.

The Smell of French Books

The smell of French books is *particulière*. It is the bloom
of favorite shoes and pillows plump
with nursing, bells
of etched glass and cream yellowing in the belly of a spoon.

The smell of French books is one candle and three cold
canvases in a crumbling room in Picardy and meadows
beyond the rusting
crucifix, pinking with puberty and wooing the mooing cows.

There is a *Livre de Poche* beside the bed. I refresh myself
with Bonnard's busy virgin in her emerald bath,
then struggle through four more pages.
Little accents fly off like perfumed arrows. From dialogue
I guess the plot and meaning of the story—
as I do in life.

I remember so little grammar, my ceremony of French books
will never change.
It is the lick, lick, lick of a chocolate clock, and I am asleep
before the chiming.

The Green Christs

I follow my great-grandfather.
He can barely walk and he can barely talk.
He is two years old.

His brother Eugène is already six. Eugène will stay here
in Belgium, and my great-grandfather will marry
a woman in Chicago whose mother wears a mantilla
before the fire in the parlor as horses clop
past toward Halsted Street.

My great-grandfather carries a soiled green bear
whose name is Lala.
The little bear's red jacket is very red and brocaded.

Eugène and his wife are buried next to the tomb
of his parents. Their names and dates are faint,
and the Christs have turned green.
Where the sun was an egg yolk and now peach, nine
sheep, one donkey and a rooster rehearse for Christmas
eve beneath an apple tree.
My great-grandfather, who last stood in this churchyard
in 1883, is buried alone
with his wife Flora near O'Hare Airport.
Only I know the graves now.

My great-grandfather and Lala stumble toward his mother.
She offers me half a plum from their garden and eats
the other half, then opens another.

She offers half to me and half to her son.
— *Shake the tree, Richard, and the fruit which falls is ripe.*
And always open a plum before tasting it.
Her fingers are stained and strong and fine. She could
play piano. A neighbor,
the soprano, begins to sing. My great-great-grandmother's
eyes, *sotto voce,* focus separately upon the bluing
and swaying.
She has Ruth's eyes, and she wears no jewelry.

Her last roses are bold and big as breakfast bowls.
She plucks a petal between a tall burgundy door
and a tall burgundy window.
— *You should have come earlier, then you would have seen them.*
They were beautiful—and everywhere.

A Rose and Its Seiche

When Daphne decided to allow her breasts
to receive mouthings, the severed Gods became alert, for her
essence could weep to the turnings
of a tongue.

Undefiled and clever, she wrapped herself
in incantations: a ruse and its worm, a rose and its seiche.

Now a deer, now a thrush nosed the vulva of a knot, and she
rose before him, and the moss of her unbound the blossom
of his lips.

Her chest became a harp and he became the other half.

Silver threads fastened their sternums, and she held his wrist
to her hip, and he rose into the god green ring.

A boar urinated down her untwining legs, tearing at new hair
indiscriminately.

Daphne tore at her hair.

There was coarseness and weeping aloud.
She concluded that speed and departure are preferable
to bark.

Once, she stopped. Her breasts stopped. The wings of her hair
fell. Her mother (who had offered her plumper body
at the time of the boar) perched,

the size and color of a heart.

Beyond the tips of Daphne's pinkness, a freckled back
strathspeyed, sprang, cartwheeled, reeled
and dashed, flipped,

flipped, flipped and leapt.

The thought—*This could be my daughter. She should have been
my daughter*—frayed her lips.

Notre Dame

A dead man bolted to a dead tree is
lodged like a bone in the throat of Notre Dame.

A tongue flickering in a lamp cannot be suppressed.

Before the burnings and conversions this choir
was a barrow where my fathers and mothers were brought
and planted like seeds in a belly.

The clerestory and blindstory were trees and each cold
intricacy, a leaf.

I forgive the bowed and kneeling patriarchs
and matriarchs separated by stone ribs, for they knew not
what they did or they were afraid or they did
know and are buried now in stone.

Before I left Chicago, I saw Auntie Jean standing
on the corner of Irving Park and Clarendon.
A squealing bus did not disturb her because she is dead.
Her coat was so old and her hat so ridiculous, I almost
hurried out to huddle her into my car,
but she wasn't
watching for me, and she wasn't
waiting for the bus like the others. She had come for her
daughter who was dying.

I have crouched in a savory cathedral like this before waiting
to be born, sipping and sleeping to the thumping
of a big bell beneath the bold
cupolas of a mother's breasts, absorbing pink stories
from windows of flesh stretched
between ribs, worming
toward a slit at the nape of the twin towers
of her knees.

Orpheus Recusant

In this widowed room I repeat
the lessons of my senescent heart,

bead by bead. I ready myself
for the opening of the bitter book

which counsels your faith
and the colored book attending

with cap and bells the approach
of our impatient story:

Attic blessed, fluted
with Lydian melancholies, the umbria
implicit in your breast

We adorn ourselves with tears and amethyst
as children of the Queen

No eclipse will ever elicit a denial
between us

This hand-pressed netting,
this veil of brides, this storied fabric winding
its whisperings about us, sleeplessly

compelling our mouths together for breath, for
birth:

I now assume Botticelli's love
for you

And if time were to abandon us in some unmeasured
embrace, I would rest beside you
until we were chosen to be brought forth again
from the cold.

Khóra Sfakia

I walk among the whores of Sfakia, the once beautiful
sons and daughters hoarding fragments, lording and ladying
and burning from the altars of their lips all instinct
still migratory.

For them the paths of scree to the promontory
decay at the turning of the sky. They hobble to the one tree
where an attendant is also a boatman and negotiate
a passage back.

I am pressed to vertical
earth, hatless, mapless and without sunglasses.
Golden bellied birds flash in a swift geometry upon lapis
lazuli, and I tremble with the thrill
of superstition: *What spirits are these*? *Whose soul cries*
from the mouth of the ass?

Now, the water is a Leviathan
and ready to swallow.
It thrashes about, not content with its containment,
neither convinced nor concerned that lungs
need land.

The whores of Sfakia wheeze and sleep with mouths open
and lamps glaring and garments pressed to their eyes.
If their messiah were to come in the night,
I could not follow, for this is not a Diaspora, and the Son
and the Father are only one half
of one God.

I wonder why the earth supports us. We expect so much
and renew so little.

It's Hero and husband, back and forth and up
and down, scattering bones of aborted destinies.
He first slurred the ancient name
of this place, Khóra Sfakia— *The whores of Sfakia,* he announced
and everyone laughed, then laughed again and laughed
all the next day.
Now, she and he and I are pinks upon the sand.

We offer our knees to the waves, and Hero calls, and her call
takes the body of a gull.
Each of us awakes from the truth of dreams to the lives
of our own making.

The sea moves her skin and enters me.
I do not fear translucence. I do not fear this pregnancy,
for I am with me.

Asleep in Ireland

My forehead touches folds and stone. It is mud
and gold. It is sky
silvered. Its curls fondle a puddle where fingers abandon
the wind to huddle as babies
at my breast.

I am asleep in a weaving field in Sligo, and the earth
mothers me.

Oh, how I love my sleep in Ireland.

All that has transpired during the previous nine years
is now a dream. When I awake
to myself unblemished,
dressed again in juniper:
I did not invite Deborah to Dublin.
We were not married in the Shelbourne Hotel.
We did not abandon the family in Wicklow,
and the family in Wicklow did not abandon me.
I did not retreat with her to Germany.
There was no divorce one year later.
I did not soil my story, and my story did not soil me.
I did not lose my adventure.

I first knelt in this dimple of nettles and puddles upon
the forty-second day of my great pilgrimage.
The sun was my shield, the fields unlettered and not dying.
I lay my bag next to this rock and lay my head
upon my bag.

I slept to the rhythm of cows
and clouds, the moon, invisible in cerulean, wandering
and blessing the shore of me
asleep upon this belly, burning with the yolks of furze
flowering into the big, dreamy, beating silence
of the embryo.

Hobo licks my palm. We walk hills wet, wax
green and valleys wetter and greener.
The sheep farmers do not concern him.
They have not yet poisoned him. He is turning away and
turning back, orange and lime
in the sun.

He is an Alsatian like me and a stray. When he died, I
buttoned him into my flannel shirt and buried him beneath
a plum tree.

We sleep now in Ireland, separated only by the vast mirror
of earth. I bite
into fruit nourished by his body. Hobo knows me
as I enter the mulberry trees.
My mother greets us from an iron chair. She rises. She, too,
is smiling victoriously. She is lantern lit, beautiful again.
I knew that she could beat the cancer.
I knew that she was still alive. I say to her,
Now, don't be upset. But there was a time I didn't know
you. Years and years when you wore your hair like this—
[*I gesture.*]
All lost. All that time is lost.
She begins to cry, but we are together again.
Before I can introduce Hobo, I awake.

I begin to move my limbs.
There is gray in my beard but I cannot see it, for I have
no mirror. I believe that I am healed.

I believe that I am healed.

All that I have dreamed is real. All that has shortened
my breath and scarred me is a dream.

With what god do I negotiate this arrangement?
And what more must I offer?

A Boat

Your toes to my bow, a knee
to your aft, my fingers inside a strap of
your camisole, your arms vining
and rubbing
with the movement of my right shoulder

I untie from my God and every god story— *Come the wind*
and the wake and the rain

Sap fattens and ovals our lips, blind
petals of a previous crossing
They are tart; they are wet
They are plum; they are asps

Look, the water is tarnished. It is the first generation
of leaves dying

Down in our belly
we are happy. We twine in the delicious
deciduous mess of our
pulp

Pregnant

I am pregnant and I am not embarrassed, and I refuse
to defend myself before the disappointed.
My babies have not been fathered by the patriarchy,
but they are not bastards.
I am not busy in commerce— I am not a landlord
or collector or provider,
but they will never be abandoned.

I am going to live in a forest where moss bathes my toes
and makes slippers for trees and pillows of stones;
I am going to deny concrete and its fumes;
I am going to swim every swell of my heart; for it is good
for my babies.
I am going to learn to not worry.
I am going to learn to listen to my fingers
and dismember every gate which does not allow the seeds
of wind and rain and light.

I am so pregnant I cannot see my feet, but my path
leads me.
When a poem comes through me, I embrace its vortex
and adore its apparitions and whisper
every word of its appendages
into song.

And when voices will no longer echo
from the bones of my back, sleep will make me a baby
in a belly again.

Dust and Light of the Dead

The wind, its wake and its rain fever the sweet and greenly
billowing, billowing.

The dust and light of the dead, those who knew us
in the blossom of our story, those who know us
as their progeny, appear
in the blind, blond wanderings of your hair.

Hurry. I hurry you
within me.
Blessings
and torments are loosed
from an interring sky. Flapping and flapping and
red, they shelter
in busy, leafing bodies.

A child
of our child, pondering this place, this leaf turning again
beneath its blossom, may
suddenly comprehend your coloring upon her
flesh.
Wherever she will spend her body, your light
will gather to her, and our sleep will remind her
of her sleep and the children
who will feed upon the milk and the dust
of her breasts.

Eulogia

Above the vindicating sea, rising whitely
from the kitchen's cold-handled blessing, her pale

cardigan flaps its green gathering
to every field

her husband remembers, forking windrows of wheat
into dry, neat breasts.
He is ancestor and self in that dust-driven moment
his red face meets
the rude wind.

Alice blue school blouses slapping
at clouds and the church
is white and the water surrounding
the forbidden

tarnishes; her skin is forgiving where the water is
silver and the ruin black as a mask
and unapproachable.

Above the weaving of their hair a branch is trembled
for a berry

as the wind would in the blond, open
field.

Where is the end room shuttered with indigo
branches?

From this throne of vernal conceit, milk cold
and bloated, bearing the fallen
spears of pine,
spines upon spines sprite green up above
the rust and mossy stream and insect
clouds—

Dear Mary, soon-to-be-forsaken, Protestant-fingered
wife, provider for the children, proceeds
from the yellow door
of the new kitchen to the tiled hall. Her blind Jack Russell,
sausage pampered, rodent wristed, bounces widely
at a sensation of sullen sunlight among the fuchsia, spins
with the grin and abandon of the closely protected.

The green-glassed porch remains narrowly open—
but only to Jack.

A fire is lit in the television room.
Down the long hall, bending to the convalescent
slope of the piebald
hill, she sweeps out each stale
fire, sending anemic wisps into a wind
frantic for the sea.

Leam of light draw near

the writhing in their salmon bodies
at the cloven

rock, lichened and forever keening, streaming,
kneeling, beaded wet and aubergine; screens of golden
leaf set glowing

the woolly sheep pounding nowhere
up the clover.
That last light steels

the partitioned windows of Johnny Byrne's
Coach & Four and the contiguous stone chapel
up to its cloistered window and the priest's
residence where Father Mahon once slept
for two weeks without a mattress, for *he*
was a just man, a generous man—not like this new
cleric, trained in England.
— *God help us. Imagine a theatrical society in Cullenglen.*
— *As if we hadn't enough nonsense—and especially with*
the youth now—
— *Well, one can see why the church is having her difficulties.*
It all started with that Vatican II.
— *I suppose he'll next be wanting to do away with the Blessed*
Sacrament itself—
— *God help us.*
— *Indeed.*

Dissembler, cast a furtive stance this side of the glass
in the hollow
bellied banqueting room: the powder of ash breaking
upon the grating, the brown bindings
and green bindings of mildewing authors, the long,

low-handled swords
impaled upon the papered wall, the palest and finest
portrait of Catherine O'Reilly—*Do you*
take this fair Aisling— I do, I do—as the light moves,
abandoning her again to the contemplative
twilight of 1914.

Cygnets amplify the sable and viridian,
insignia of faith, for the fading
shall not be forgotten, not here. This night
they awaken to the ripple of Niamh's

mirror. Here is the bright field
of their gathering, and the shrill
of the silence is the sound of their chorus,
the memory of an intonation, the little whistles

and green stories, their prayers we repeat
in the gethsemane of our hearts.

Twin cygnets, darlings of the water darkling,
what do you know beyond the reflection

of the low stone bridge—

In the Watery Place

When Iris met Dorothy they did not chirp. They did not
assume wings or daring saffron breasts
as they do to revive the restive
in this watery
place.

They met the midnight after the fifth anniversary of my
mother's death. The vessel of your mother
lay beneath blankets of frozen rose
arrangements
only six
days.

Beneath our plumped coverlet, I held your hand. Snow
pewtered and powdered the indigo
hours. Our mothers hovered,
wide as the ceiling,
looking into the room
as if it were a
cradle.

The Single, Sacred Body

A coldly assisted immersion segregated your first
prettiness, each tendril, the mouth and eyes and blind thighs
of an oblation.

Florentines once determined the orient of your neck.
They robed you in snow and vermilion, and you were
pleasing to prelates. Prelates and postulants
surround you still—but they do not sustain you
or protect you.

Saints positioned along a scalloped wall
recognize fear;
they hear us say, *I have never loved like this before,*
and I shall never love like this again—but their bodies
are plaster and azure.
They have been martyred; and I have chosen to abandon
their kingdom.

Before you turn and offer your neck, your twin
leaps back.
Her lip is uncertain and her eyes
hesitate. The tips of your fingers are cold
and kind as her hair sweeps back
against the glass. I remove the other dumb glove
to entrance every finger, but we are condemned to separate
monopolies which require less and less
light. This exile must be a punishment
for having offered our lips
to strangers.

I cannot learn to love the lost hours.

Every fluted pillar, every iridescence between branches
prophesied you. Your breasts restore me to the first
and last face
of God.

Do not fear this exodus.
Angels escort us and adorn us
as adorable siblings.

Our love will confound all vain idols
of commerce and compromise,
for we have been chosen to demonstrate
the single, sacred body.

The Caretaker

The striped shawl represents the embrace of the Deity.
The man in glass is a Hebrew; the big, Biblical beard
and Palestine-pink turban
allow no other interpretation. His fine leather boots
are an artist's invention, a handsome, Cossack
(and, therefore, ridiculous) affectation.

Here in the hall of remembrances where my heels are dull,
little lamps amber like seeds of flickering souls
down a Saxon throat. Behind the door to the vaulted portico
a dark girl strains

to a flaxen boy. He presses her back until she is stained
Tigris green. The story of Helen does not belong
to this Genesis, but there should be
a place among all these zealots for a woman who is
scintillating and not immaculate.
Good. It is good that she strains to enter.

I steady myself with my lesson: *Better to be alone and whole*
than to mislead the heart of another; and in that
conciliatory moment, I unlock a door
for a woman and her consort wandering toward the crypt.

I have seen them in the sanctuary emboldened by a flourish
of brass and blue incense. The nave is their domain.
He has paid for the privilege.
I wonder, *Why have they come here, below?*

He is not so handsome now; and the animal she carries—
which is her body—is hungry
for a hunter. The ridges of her pushing through
silk torment my mouth.
I would remove all rings and stones, for I want her fingers
naked as lips. And she wants her fingers naked, too.
Her clouded, tightening eyes

confess this. But Ruth is watching.
She rises from sheaves and doves and nipples of white
clusters as she does every night.
Her glass eyes allow no blubbering. *Who shall ascend*

the mountain of the Lord and who shall stand in His holy place?
My mother would hold my left hand in her right
and my sister's right hand in her left as we repeated together,
He who has clean hands and a pure heart.
I may not believe in the God of these coloring book
windows, but I want clean hands.

Ruthie kept every one of my letters, bound with an amethyst
ribbon. She opened them one white morning. We reclined
upon her pink pillows
beside the ribbon as if it had come from her body;
and though I followed that purple tongue back into its nest,
I never wanted more of her.

I never loved her childhood, the slim shoes she wore to work
or the red toes which widened the shoes, her plumping
fingers or the way they unsettled suddenly
gray hairs from her forehead.

We could go free, she once invoked, the flags of her feet high
above our body. *We could*

heal each other. Now, after I lock each door and extinguish
every lamp, I face a mirror
and brush and brush, spitting white foam
from my mouth.

Epiphany in the Afternoon

When your breasts were fruit I climbed until I bled

Clouds suppled, separating from the Sternum, and choirs
flooded my lungs lofting as
clouds

Here are your colors: Asiatic pink and jaundice,
prolonged pansy, purpling
cobalt, Roman
lace, pomegranate, tongue tip, fig, quince, violence, rain, wine,
bruise,
bone, sun, yawn

Knees offer your mouth of blood in silk as confection

Evora (A Song)

In Evora there is a church
and the church was once a mosque
and the mosque was once a church
and the church was once a temple in the time the Romans

Behind the altar there is a false tomb
and beneath a Christian name there are thousands of years
of roots writhing through stone
and water echoes up vertebrae which must have been steps
and its light is the juice of emeralds

Now, consider the well that is my throat
and the pool that is my chest

What does one do when a well has been capped
for so many generations?
Is water safe in the stomach?

How did I become addicted to a self-imposed periphery,
its tithes, its prick and its poison?
Can all of this be unlearned in one generation,
one season, one summer?

My grandfathers and grandmothers
and their grandparents meet for the first time in me
I carry them to familiar places
I am their hands, their thighs, their nose
their eyes, their lips, their teeth, their tongue

How did I become addicted to a self-imposed periphery,
its tithes, its prick and its poison?
Can all of this be unlearned in one generation,
one season, one summer?

I am the voice and the body now
and all that is closed will be opened
and all that hurts will be repaired
and all that sleeps without dreaming will be green again

In Evora there is a church
Inside the church there is a tomb
and inside the tomb there is a cistern
and inside the cistern there is water
and its light is the juice of emeralds

Anyone Who Journeys

Anyone who journeys this far south, stays in Essaouira long enough to wash underclothes under a cold-water tap in a room Gaughin yellow and indigo tiled, follows the sun slanting trail of Portuguese portals from Bab Lachour to Café Essalem to Café Petite France, decides *enfin* to become a writer.

Perhaps, it is the lure of a private, Bible-black bound journal and ink pen; one elbow on the table; a glass of coffee and hot milk crusted with cinnamon; a glass of water, pure as a prism—untouched; sugar cubes—untouched; an aluminum spoon rivaling silver from a saucer coffee stained, ovaled by equatorial light; intent eyes, the second sip; returning to appropriate a next phrase of wild, little, many-lettered, many-legged words on the vast, white terrain of another page.

Perhaps, it is simply having something to do, coffee after coffee, a short-term purpose—a stick in the earth, a stone, a shadow stick measuring the virginal procession of minutes.

Only Dennis does not want to write. He is from the isle of Jersey; his family has money; and he has no ambition this winter. Happily he sits sipping with 800 pages of Dickens beneath the striped cone of a straw hat bargained for in the suq, the serpentine alleys stinking of piss and smoke, leather, lavender, essences of peppermint, wood shavings, lemon wood, cinnamon, cinders, orange, blood and blood red spices behind us.

We face the salt and froth of the sea, each man wearing a silly hat covering eyes and nose. The women wear dark glasses.

Abdou Khadar does not wear a hat; he is Moroccan. He smokes Marlboro filters. He has his shoes polished for two dirhams by the child with scarred cheeks and jaundiced eyes.

He breathes blue smoke: "Two years I have these shoes—," raising them, shining shoes to the sun.

Robyn, Londoner, junior film editor, adjusts, readjusts the soiled brim of a safari cap: "Abdul, Dennis et moi avons une idée. Nous voudrons—"

"Voudrions—"

"Nous voudrions...une librairie...."

"You're English. Speak English."

"We want to make—to organize a sort of library for travelers to exchange books." Robyn's neck blushes to the mouth of the striped sailor shirt Dennis wore yesterday to the hamam. His left wrist, cluttered luxuriantly with ornamental bangles, is darker than his hair, shagged summer blond, unwashed.

Unwashed, Kitty, psychiatric nurse from Bristol, sunburning her nose, says: "With my books, I suppose."

"Where?" [Iris] "Where?"

"Here, where we're sitting. For an hour every day. Right, Dennis?"

"No money."

"No, it's not for that purpose, Abdul."

"Be careful. I tell you, be careful. Life is not so open here. The owner of the café—he's Mafia. *If* he agrees, then someone else—someone who walks around to look at things—sees what you're doing, and then in two, three days there's trouble, perhaps."

"But it's not illegal—"

"But who needs this. You want a book I have, ask me." Abdou grins to a chorus of placid faces seeking or avoiding the sun.

"Why make things different? We are sitting here; here is the sun; no one bothers anyone—," Ute deranging her prawn pink day pack for a slim, teal blue tin of Nivea.

My face is distended in two, large, blue lenses. I yearn for her substantial *Death in Venice.*

Kitty lifts and lowers her chin as if securing a violin: "*Nicholas Nickleby* does not go into this library."

Dennis, fisherman red, raises a British grimace.

Martin's bad eye wanders enthusiastically. He motions to the waiter: half coffee, half milk. "It will rain today or tomorrow."

"How do you know?" Kitty thrusts her punished nose to a last slat of virile light. "How do you know?"

A muezzin erupts from a football field loudspeaker. Abdou snaps open a brushed-chrome lighter, laughs, tap tap taps the tip of a fresh cigarette to the table, mulatto-milk puddled: "Merde."

"Like a Virgin" is cut midchorus. Allah confuses all conversation. Veiled women walking in threes are vindicated.

We survey the square, we veterans of the seaport town.

David unbuttons his shirt to graying, ginger-freckled breasts. He was here in '68. He remembers Hendrix at Diabat.

"Did you notice how quiet it is today? The police arrested all the hustlers—first thing this morning. There was a fight between seven dealers last night. Someone was killed in the Kasbah Sqala. Hari told me. Now, there's no hash anywhere. It's dry as Iowa. Everyone's going to Marrakech."

"When?" Martin mouths.

"I don't care." Clea slurs fig liquor into her coffee.

"Ah, the airport authors!" spits Kamel of the leather shop through belt brown teeth.

Christopher and Chloe, Catholics from New Jersey, wrapped as Berber twins, guide a rust red bicycle strapped with striped, cornucopian baskets.

Iris: "Do you realize that child cooks every meal—"

Kitty: "He's a swine. He was a swine last year, and he's a swine this year. Does he still varnish his fingernails? I'm sure Père Claude must find that *most* interesting."

Ute chortles.

Clea's cough ruminates into a rattle. "There are only two questions, David: Did you have a happy childhood? and What is your birthsign?" Tap, tap [spoon to glass].

"Well?" Ute's lips remain parted.

"Scorpio. And my childhood was *very* abusive."

"No, not you, David." Her cigarette is delicious. "You're a Leo, aren't you?"

David purrs.

Hari prowls toward our table, untangling hennaed hair oiled into long ringlets.

Clea holds large, laboratory white teeth together approximating a smile. A fine middle finger steadies predatory glasses.

The young Moroccans watch us. They do not understand this wandering from café to café. In the heat they cross to Mogador, the purple island, or camp in Diabat at the end of the crescent of hot sand. Why just sit like that all day, they wonder, with the little books and cheap pens?

But they know nothing of Hemingway or moveable feasts or the pleasures of lost generations.

Abduction

Rain be our witness.

This elegant curtain of serpents and cypress-tongued moons
has fed upon your youth.

Place sorrow to the prow.
Forsake each barren tomb:
Your fury could propel a sky of pounding bells, and the single
leaves that follow will gather again at your wrist.

Beyond the censure of torches, as the hold
of your indigo hands
approximates my furrowing, a scion of our soul is born
into the wand of your body: *Lay it to the folds of my ribs*
where your hair weaves its mysteries and your feet mouth
their fragrance.

You bleed and bleed distress from the bruise at your breast,
and still, the voice
in your throat is the instruction of your husband, wrestling
back any menstruation to birth
the dominion of his flat, frenzied arms.

I bite at his repository. You instruct me, finger by
finger.

You are charting and marking the course of my exasperation,
aren't you, jonquil lips?

A bitten lip counsels, *Sleep*. A turning leaf admonishes,
Decide.
I seep through drape, briar and bone. The murmur and flavor
of our blood change.
Your wings become sleeker and quicker.

Choirs of blatant, unblanketed knees unfold
to our passing, but no remedy
rises from the river, no promise of myrtle and rain-plumped
roses is prepared to palliate their fading.

The ascendant sky feeds upon their pallor and that light is
gathered to you.

Digging Up the Cancer Field

What poisons caw from the red well
of the chest.

My meadow, my June bed,
torn back, doubled back as a carpet, reveals
worms big as shrimp turning and churning and bursting
open to multiply. And I recognize in this busy seeding
operation my mother's
cancer.

I beseech the sun, *Burn them.*
I beseech the moon, *Sicken them.*
I beseech and beseech, but I must rip each
from its roots.
My chest, my acre, becomes scorched aisles of white lips,
working to eliminate this multitude of angry, little machines
delirious for abuse.

So many generations seeding
into me, *Why have you given me this.* I must make
our domain clean again. Tender as new skin. Flinching from
the touch, pink and burning clean.

Mother knew. She dug at her skin.
Poor, dear mother, you bled our mythology
of heroes and deities.

You became creator
and model

and marble.
In death you lay blond
as a crusader upon a draped table, shorn and distorted
and shrouded for planting.
I pressed
my forehead to your forehead,
I now assume your contest, this sanctification, this remaking,
this purification of self, this digging
up the cancer field.

In the Rose of Our Thigh

We were the anointed. We made whole
that which was separate.
On our second day

our fingers formed
rosettes, glowing
and closing and
glowing up above

the cherry lights and little
snow lights tinkling
from trees leafing
and ice raptured.
We were that clean,

so finely spun,
vernal
and gilt, lit
as a gift
from a God.

I know that you hurt
and curse as your red heels
click across the cold
vaulting of each lost
communion.

Between these pillows
you were a river of lapis
lazuli and I foamed forth
a delirious sky.
No dangling
food pregnant with pink
seeds was more
delicious than yours.
Even the Creator
of cold, who fondles
all emerald things until they are
ashen, hesitated over this

bed, for His worm's
winding
and unwinding
did not taste
in the rose of our thigh.

Per Viam ad Vitam

Here is a filament of your hair pressed
to the cup of my hand, precious

in sunlight, protected from capricious, curious
winds.

Here the impetuous once stood,
cloaked in mellifluent tongues at this confluence
of limbs.

Orange offerings perfused her legs.
A pressing together of lips left their verdigris
upon her wrist: *Adore me*
with lives

lapin
white

milk

teeth
tinkling

swollen

silk
of a maiden's furtive
thread

I kiss each fingertip painted Marian pink. I abhor
the color but taste the mouth at your knees, twining
with envious sea grass, narcissus incarnate
broken to the breast
among siblings of lime and sable
green light: *In that slender season all was impatient*
for our lungs.

When the first apostles came and struck the painted head
from the white breasted
body, the impotent rejoiced at this
pool.
Turtles (darting still) remember their dippings
and shiverings.

Dust blew to the face and the water
was never turquoise again.

At a distant summons of horns you sit,
pour, consider white-lipped
leaves, mahogany mirrored.
Your fingers (fashioned for Gothic adoration) shorten
to the breath
of a child in a room of little whispers.
I do not implore.
Between that petulant door and a mother's narrow
mirror, clouded with cut
blossoms and silver blossoms, the Son assumes
his pewter ascendancy.

You sacrifice, I
know, to that god, withering mouth
to mouth, his disgrace about your neck, *Te Deum,*
Te Deum and the tedium of disguise.

I kneel to embrace the child we know in our fingers
entwined at the lip
of the white pool where spirits
unharnessed seek the one
importunate tongue.

The Absolute of Indigo

This mosaic of mesmerized silver
fish and chartreuse
scum harboring
seed pods
sailed all green things once
to the young peninsulas

of my lungs.

I was held to this stone
hundreds of fish years ago.
My mother warmed me and warned me; but
an emerald billowed up and
I skipped ahead, popping and twinkling
as a skiff's pennant, a tin of spinach
pressed to my biceps, and I begged my mom

not to be afraid.

All things are arranged now in my vessel.
I hear her. She whispers, *Do not worry*, as she passes,
bludgeoned
with twilight, into the absolute
of indigo.